To Maddie, Denney, i l ....
Three wonderful :
who are GREAT fam.

Love,
Paul

SHERLOCK
McBIES Kit

SHERLOCK McBISKIT

Shares His Secrets To Good Character And Respect

~ by Pauli Reading ~

SHERLOCK McBISKIT & FRIENDS COMPANY

~ BOOK ONE ~

SHERLOCK McBISKIT

Shares His Secrets
To Good Character And Respect

Sherlock McBiskit and Friends Company
Post Office Box 12325
Charlotte, N.C. 28220
sherlockmcbiskit@sherlockmcbiskit.com
http://sherlockmcbiskit.com

All rights reserved. No part of this book may be reproduced or trans-
mitted in any form or by any means, electronic or mechanical, including
photocopying, recording, or by any information storage and retrieval
system, without permission from the author, except for the inclusion of
brief quotations in a review.

Copyright © 2008 by Pauli Reading

First Edition ISBN
Hardcover 978-0-9816193-4-7

First Edition 2008
Printed in These United States of America

Library of Congress Cataloging-in-Publication
Data Control Number 2008903356

ACKNOWLEDGEMENTS

BASED ON THE WISDOM AND TEACHINGS
OF
VEGA ROZENBERG

MASTER HEALER AND TEACHER

WORLD RENOWNED ALCHEMIST
OF PERSONAL EVOLUTION

SPECIAL THANKS TO:

Tracy and Ali Reading
for their support and integrity

Robert and Gertrude Scharff
for their lessons on the importance of good character

Judith Fain
for her unwavering love and encouragement

Shirley Reading
for her great work as a literary agent

Angie Underwood
partner, BookCoverPro Book Design Software,
for designing the cover

Debbie Filz
for her illustrations and layout design

HELLO THERE!

Lads and lassies! How do you do?

I am Sherlock McBiskit with lots to teach you!

Oh, you might think, I am just a wee little dog,

But when you get to know me,

You won't think that at all.

I am a powerful canine, you soon will see.

I will teach you to be powerful, just like me!

So, now come with me, and I will tell you my tale.

We'll have lots of fun, and through life,

        You'll learn to sail.

Whatever the problem, what I teach can help fix it.

Sure as my name is **SHERLOCK McBISKIT!**

I have learned many secrets to having a good life,

Where you get lots of riches and lose lots of strife.

"How did you learn these secrets?" of me, you might ask.

Finding someone to teach me was quite a big task.

I searched and searched for someone to show me the way.

A man wiser than wise, I found on one special day.

On top of a very tall mountain, he does live,

And excellent advice he is able to give.

You might ask,

"What is his name, this man that lives high?"

Oh, he is named after the **BRIGHTEST** star in the sky!

Here is the first secret that most people don't know.

Life gives us lots of tests. I will tell you it's so.

    These challenges are not bad.

        They are not wrong.

Life sends us these tests to make us very strong!

Each test we pass, a door opens and we go through.

The more **POWERFUL** we become!

The more we **CAN DO!**

So, never fear a challenge that may come your way.

Just face it and go through it -

ON TO A BETTER DAY!

My wise teacher taught me how to pass all life's tests.

"Use **GOOD CHARACTER**, as you journey on your quest.

This means acting in a way that is

GOOD FOR YOU AND OTHERS.

If you do, you will pass all the tests, my brother."

"But, it is not all about acting, this is true.

For this is a way of

THINKING,

the whole day through!"

TRAINING YOUR BRAIN

"To do this, little Sherlock, you **MUST** train your brain.

Your brain won't like this, it will think it's a pain.

When the brain wants to do something that is not right,

You must yell loud **NO!** and put up a good fight!

You may have to yell,
　　　　　　NO!
　　　　　　　　OVER
　　　　　　　　　　AND
　　　　　　　　　　　　OVER
　　　　　　　　　　　　　　AGAIN!

Now, do not worry, you will win in the end.

When you yell **NO!** The brain for a moment will stop.

You will pull out the bad thoughts and put in a new crop.

Over the brain you will become quite a **KING!**

Whenever a test comes, you will pass **EVERYTHING!**"

MY FIRST LIFE TEST

My first test came when I was just a little guy.

To my Mom and Dad dog, I had to say goodbye.

I am from Scotland, a country across the sea,

And I had to travel **FAR** to my new family.

I was very sad until I remembered the tests.

Then, I knew this would be good.

This would be for the **BEST!**

My new family was quite kind, loving, and good,

But I knew I'd have to work hard,

                  OH YES! YES! I WOULD!

They were very human you see, not canine like me.

Their thinking was **SO** different!
                                        OH
                                                YES!
                                                          YES!
                                                                      SIREE!

I thought more like a wolf which is not bad in the wild,

But this would not work for my new Mom, Dad, and their child.

To pass this test, **GOOD CHARACTER** I must use.

If I did not, I was going to surely lose!

RESPECT

My new Mom said, "Respect you must learn and know.

Treating others with high regard is the way to go."

I first had to learn to respect her as my teacher.

She said, "You must Sherlock, or I won't be able to reach ya'.

You must look at me always, when I am speaking.

It is how I can teach you the knowledge you are seeking."

"Looking at someone when they talk is important for sure.

To understand humans, this will be your first door."

But, I
        DID
                NOT
                      WANT
                              TO!

        THERE WAS SO MUCH TO SEE!

Out the window there were

        BIRDS! TWO MICE!

            and

        ONE BUMBLEBEE!

My mom yelled,

"SHERLOCK!

NO! NO! NO! NO! NO!"

I stopped for a second and told my brain - WHOA!

I turned around and looked at her face.

She gave me a treat, which I jumped up to taste.

Now, whenever at me, my Mom begins talking,

I look at her. I stop playing, running, or walking.

Because I look at her, she has taught me a ton!

    Like how to live with humans,

        Which is now **MUCH** more fun!

When others are talking to you, at them, **ALWAYS** look.

You'll learn **LOTS** of things, training my brain is all it took.

To look at someone when they talk is a life test.

IT IS GOOD FOR YOU AND OTHERS,

SO YOU KNOW IT IS BEST!

RESPECT PROPERTY

The next thing I learned was to respect the things I own.

This means to respect **EVERYTHING** - not just my bone.

Here is a story about how I made a mistake.

I'll tell you, so it is one you will learn not to make.

    My Mom she is a **VERY, VERY** nice lady.

She brought me home a nice stuffed animal baby.

First thing I did was tear off it's head, eyes, and **NOSE!**

Then, went on to eat it's tail, arms, and **TOES!**

Oh, my mom was not pleased but gave me another.

I tore it up again which angered my mother.

She said, **"No More for you! Sherlock McBiskit!"**

Oh No! I thought. **I better find a way to fix it!**

    "Oh Please! Please!" I cried,

        "Please, Give me another try!

It is not fun without one! **I THINK I MIGHT DIE!"**

"Now Sherlock," she said,

"I will give you just **ONE** more."

I took such good care of it, she gave me another **FOUR!**

I now have a whole stuffed animal collection.

Since I take care of them, they look like perfection!

Now, **PLEASE** remember to respect all you have got.

If you don't, you might end up not having a lot!

Taking care of your things is a life test.

IT IS GOOD FOR YOU AND OTHERS,

SO YOU KNOW IT IS BEST!

Manners was the next lesson of respect to learn.

Be careful with your mouth or you may get burned.

For I once thought it fun to misbehave and to tease.

Why was it important to say,

"THANK YOU" and **"PLEASE?"**

This lesson I learned not from my Mom or my Dad.

I learned this from a golden retriever named Tad.

My mom walks me around our neighborhood each day.

I come across Tad when I have gone about half way.

Tad sits on his porch and basks in the morning sun.

How boring, I thought. Let me have a little fun,

"HEY TAD!

YOUR FACE IS SO VERY WRINKLED AND GRAY!

I BET YOU ARE WAY TOO OLD TO CHASE ME TODAY!"

My Mom would say, "Sherlock! It is awful to tease!

STOP IT! STOP IT! STOP IT! RIGHT NOW!

I MEAN RIGHT NOW!

PLEASE!"

Oh, but how I really, really liked my little game.

Then, Tad made me realize, I was being QUITE A PAIN!

One day, I began my teasing and chatter,

And on this day, Tad had enough of this matter.

"Young lad, you think yourself to be funny and cool.

But, what you are doing, makes you look like a **FOOL!**

Yes, I may very well look old, wrinkled, and gray,

But, if you get to know me, you should see how I play!"

"I know **MANY** places here to have fun and play games!"

"I have **LOTS** of Friends like -

POODLES!

SHEEPDOGS!

AND

GREAT DANES!"

"**M**y friends and I have watched your teasing for a while.

I'll tell you, it doesn't make even one of us smile.

It is why we have not let you join in our clan.

Making fun of others is a practice we **MUST** ban!

If you can be careful with what you do and say,

    We would **LOVE** for you to

    COME AND PLAY WITH US TODAY!"

"**YES! YES!**" I said.

"**I AM SORRY! PLEASE FORGIVE!**

To tease others is **NOT** the way I want to live!

I would **VERY MUCH** like to have some fun dog friends!

I **PROMISE** the teasing from **THIS DAY ON ENDS!**"

So, from that day until now, with my mouth I take care.

I **ALWAYS** think before I speak, I know this is fair.

"THANK YOU! THANK YOU!"

To the golden retriever named Tad.

Without his advice, a lonely life I would have had.

To use your mouth wisely is also a life test.

IT IS GOOD FOR YOU AND OTHERS,

SO YOU KNOW IT IS BEST!

There is someone else I would like to mention…

Someone people forget, though it's not their intention.

It is someone you are with every day and every night.

It's someone you **NEVER** let out of your sight!

Who is this someone? Can you tell? Can you say?

Yes, it is **YOU!** that you must respect **EVERY DAY!**

Just like you speak to and do good things for others,

Do those same things for **YOURSELF!** my sisters and brothers.

When you respect and take care of **YOURSELF** each day.

You can do more for others in **EVERY** way!

To respect yourself is also a life test.

IT IS GOOD FOR YOU AND OTHERS,

SO YOU KNOW IT IS BEST!

It's time for me to tell you lads and lassies goodbye.

Promise me these few things I told you, you will try.

Respect others, like your teachers, friends, Moms, and Dads,

Sisters, brothers, even golden retrievers named Tad!

Look at them when they talk to you, and speak to them nice.

Train your brain to do this.

BEFORE YOU SPEAK, THINK TWICE!

Respect all things you have and take care of them well.

I know you will, because you are **ALL** smart. I can tell.

Don't forget to respect that most important - **YOU!**

Because you are -

VERY SPECIAL and **WONDERFUL** too!

FAREWELL!

And **ALWAYS** remember life gives us lots of tests.

They are to make us stronger, and are for the **BEST!**

There is only one way to pass the tests, you see.

Thinking and acting with **GOOD CHARACTER** is the key!

I've enjoyed being with you, but guess for now that's it.

Love to all of you from Me -

SHERLOCK McBISKIT

THE END!

Pauli Reading resides in Charlotte, North Carolina with her husband, daughter, and **Sherlock McBiskit**. She has taught Character Education to thousands of elementary school students accompanied by **Sherlock McBiskit** and many other canine friends.

Please visit Pauli Reading and Sherlock McBiskit on
The Sherlock McBiskit & Friends website
HTTP://WWW.SHERLOCKMCBISKIT.COM

To order copies of SHERLOCK McBISKIT:

(internet orders)
http://www.sherlockmcbiskit.com

(email orders)
sherlockmcbiskit@sherlockmcbiskit.com

(postal orders)
Sherlock McBiskit & Friends Company
P.O. Box 12325
Charlotte, N.C. 28220